Old Provincetown
IN EARLY PHOTOGRAPHS

Irma Ruckstuhl

DOVER PUBLICATIONS, INC.
NEW YORK

ACKNOWLEDGMENTS

Stanley Snow, son of the late Louis Snow, encouraged and supported this project and helped in identifying some previously unknown subjects in his father's photographs. Mr. Snow and his wife Dorothy also conveyed to me their deep admiration and respect for the elder Mr. Snow and his memory. My special thanks to Hilary Bamford, a longtime friend who shares with me a fascination for old things and who kindly permitted me unlimited access to her large and varied collection of Provincetowniana.

Captain Charles Mayo, a third-generation Provincetown native, generously recounted some of his reminiscences of the East End and the waterfront, and shared his considerable knowledge of fishing and sailing vessels.

Lurana Cook, coauthor of *Provincetown Massachusetts Cemetery Inscriptions*, always had the answer when the question dealt with the genealogy of Provincetown families.

NOTE

In the early 1900s the numbering of houses along Commercial Street was changed. No common factor was used in making the change and it is not possible to determine the new number of a house by addition or subtraction. However, all even numbers in the old system appear to be on the south or water side of Commercial Street; the reverse is now true.

All of the numbers cited here are the *old numbers.*

Published in Canada by General Publishing Company, Ltd., 30 Lesmill Road, Don Mills, Toronto, Ontario.
Published in the United Kingdom by Constable and Company, Ltd.

Old Provincetown in Early Photographs is a new work, first published by Dover Publications, Inc., in 1987.

Book design by Carol Belanger Grafton
Manufactured in the United States of America
Dover Publications, Inc., 31 East 2nd Street, Mineola, N.Y. 11501

Library of Congress Cataloging-in-Publication Data

Ruckstuhl, Irma M.
    Old Provincetown in early photographs.

    Bibliography: p.
    Includes index.
    1. Provincetown (Mass.)—Description—Views. 2. Provincetown (Mass.)—History—Pictorial works. I. Title.
F74.P96R83   1987   974.4'92   86-32953
ISBN 0-486-25410-0

Introduction

In 1936, Mary Heaton Vorse described Provincetown as "forever changing—forever changeless." Her observation seems as apt today, 50 years later. The town is still three and a half miles long and two streets wide and its profile, seen from the water, is still remarkably similar to the harbor views in these early photographs. These images do not provide a comprehensive history of Provincetown. Rather, they capture a brief period in the everyday life of a town at the time when it was beginning a steady shift from economic dependence on fishing and seafaring to summer tourism. Shortly before the turn of the century, Provincetown was the most populous town on Cape Cod, with nearly 4500 inhabitants. There were more than 250 ships, including Grand Bankers, whalers and coasters, more than 50 wharves, two trains a day in each direction to and from Boston. Today it has fewer than 30 fishing vessels, two commercial wharves, no trains and a summer population, including transients, variously estimated at between 30,000 and 45,000.

Situated at the tip of Cape Cod, a peninsula stretching like a bent arm about 60 miles into Massachusetts Bay, Provincetown is surrounded by the sea and sand dunes and has never had the luxury of space for expansion. Instead, it has grown by becoming denser—former lawns and gardens are now covered by buildings which have themselves been enlarged in all directions, even subterraneously. Spacious homes have been divided into apartments or become guesthouses, and there is scarcely a house in the busy central area that does not contain at least one shop, restaurant or other commercial establishment. Despite all this, and a summer inundation of automobiles, for most of the year Provincetown still feels like the small town it really is, albeit a considerably more sophisticated place than might be expected of a community of 3500 permanent residents. No one who comes into contact with Provincetown seems unaffected by it. Visitors either love it or hate it and there is a tendency for many on the rest of the Cape to pretend or wish it did not exist. For those of us who have chosen to call it home, it also often provokes a similar love-hate relationship. It can be infuriating, frustrating, but there is no other place quite like it.

Almost every schoolchild has been taught that the Pilgrims landed at Plymouth. Actually, the *Mayflower* first made land in the New World on November 11 (old style), 1620 in Provincetown Harbor. That same day, the men of the company drew up and signed a compact for the government of the colony—a document considered the first popularly drawn written constitution adopted in America. They explored the area on foot as far as present-day Wellfleet, but found it unsuitable for farming and left on November 20 for Plymouth.

For about 100 years after that, it is believed the Lower Cape was primarily the transient residence of a rough group of fishermen, smugglers and looters of shipwrecks who lived during the summers on Long Point in a settlement known as Helltown, returning each autumn to the Plymouth area. By 1727, however, there was enough of a permanent population to incorporate the Town of Provincetown. Virtually surrounded by water, its development alternately prospered and waned because of its vulnerable and exposed situation. It was badly affected by the Revolutionary War, when the British used the harbor as the main port for their blockading fleet. Only after the War of 1812 did the area settle into a prolonged period of prosperity, reaching its zenith in the 1850s–1870s, when the town led all the others on Cape Cod with the largest fleet of fishing and whaling ships, catching twice the total of the others combined. Remarkably, scarcely ten years later, the industry had nearly collapsed, the result of a lack of fish, a change from the consumption of salted to fresh fish and the substitution of other fuels for whale oil.

During this period the town's population also changed dramatically, from a nearly homogeneous group of Yankee stock, by the addition of nearly 2000 Portuguese, many of whom had come to America as crews on whaling vessels. Excellent fishermen and seafarers, they settled down and their descendants now form the major part of the year-round population.

As fishing declined, the town was rediscovered by summer tourists and artists, who then, as now, relish the incomparable beaches, the remarkable quality of its light, the charm of its narrow streets and hodgepodge of houses and buildings and its tolerant atmosphere.

The names and work of only four early photographers in Provincetown are known: George H. Nickerson, William M. Smith, Irving Rosenthal and Louis Snow. Nickerson was born in Centerville, Massachusetts, in 1835 and served in the infantry during the Civil War, emerging with the rank of lieutenant. It is likely that his was the first photographic studio in Provincetown. In 1880, when he was 45, he entered partnership with William Smith, who was then in his early twenties. They worked together for three years out of rooms on the third floor of the public library, producing a large number of local stereograph views that bear their names. When they parted, Mr. Nickerson moved his establishment to "first door east of post office" and advertised "lifesize crayons a speciality," and "headquarters for Cape Cod views."

Mr. Smith took over the premises at 341 Commercial Street nearly opposite the First National Bank, purchasing the property in 1889. He solicited "copying and enlarging from old tintypes," as well as other photographic work. Mr. Smith left Provincetown around the turn of the century and did not reestablish his business when he returned some years later. He died in 1943.

Mr. Nickerson died in 1890 of heart disease, leaving "a widow and a little adopted daughter." Irving Rosenthal, who was managing the Nickerson studio at that time, succeeded to the business. Unlike Nickerson, Smith and Rosenthal, Louis Snow did not rely on photography as his primary source of income. His grandfather Obadiah, a boatbuilder, was also organist and choirmaster at the Center Methodist Church. In about 1873, with his son Olin, he began a business as a dealer in music, pianos, organs and other house furnishings at 250 Commercial Street. Obadiah died in 1906 at the age of 81, followed only three years later by Olin, who succumbed to pneumonia after working with wet feet in the family's cranberry bog. He was 58, and his son Louis took over the running of the business. The store was agent for the Emerson Piano Co. of Boston and Louis learned piano tuning at the factory. He also played violin for many years with a local dance orchestra every Friday night and could also do an excellent job as a paperhanger for customers who purchased the shop's wallpapers.

According to Louis's son Stanley, a retired officer of the First National Bank of Provincetown, although Louis was listed in a local business directory in 1901 as a photographer and did take

commissions for photographic work, his interest in the field was mainly as a hobby. He had two cameras with large tripods (models unknown), a lens that cost $100 "back in those days" (perhaps the Zeiss mentioned on one of his envelopes) and his own darkroom. "He was a perfectionist in everything he did," remembers Stanley. When he died in 1963, two months short of his ninety-first birthday, he left hundreds of glass-plate negatives, neatly labeled in manila sleeves. A large selection of them was given by the family (another son, Morris, lives with his wife in Largo, Florida) to the Provincetown Historical Association, some to the National Park Service for their exhibition at the Eastham headquarters of the Cape Cod National Seashore and some to John Bell, a family friend with a deep interest in local history.

Mr. Bell used a number of the photographs to illustrate a column, "Alongshore," which he wrote for the *Provincetown Advocate* in the 1960s and had hoped to use them in a book which would compare the old photographs with pictures of the sites as they appear now. But his health deteriorated and in 1981, knowing my interest in Provincetown lore, he offered the Snow collection to me. Mr. Bell died in 1983. Though this work does not take the form he envisioned, I feel he would be pleased to know that the photographs he appreciated so greatly will now be readily available; those people interested in comparing present-day views with those of nearly a century ago can do so easily.

Identification of locations and people has been made from Louis Snow's own descriptions on the envelopes holding the plates, John Bell's research and my own detailed examination of many contemporary books and newspaper accounts. These sources sometimes conflict and, although every attempt has been made to be scrupulously accurate, some errors may be present.

There is no question that Provincetown in summer is now a different place than it used to be, but is there anywhere in the world about which this cannot be said? Some date the change to the establishment of the Cape Cod National Seashore, some to the construction of the Mid-Cape Highway, others to cheap air travel. No doubt all of these factors have contributed to the era of mass tourism on the Cape. When these photographs were taken, Provincetowners were probably lamenting the changes caused by the decline of whaling and "fish-making" (the preparation of dried salt cod) and the lack of a market for sea salt. Presently, the Cape is undergoing another profound change: Its population is shifting heavily to retirees (in parts of the Upper Cape to city-bound commuters), while the condominium craze is changing the look of the traditional Cape towns. A finite supply of water and other environmental factors may limit the growth of the Cape, but technological advances may overcome these problems too, and there is now serious concern that the very attributes attracting people to the Cape will soon be destroyed. Perhaps those of us still around 50 years from now will look at photos of the 1960s–1980s with the same sort of affectionate and wistful nostalgia with which we view these pictures taken by Louis Snow almost a century ago.

IRMA RUCKSTUHL
Provincetown

Contents

On the Road to Provincetown

1. The Marconi Wireless Station at Wellfleet. Early transatlantic radio messages were sent from the station. Seen here ca. 1903, the station was abandoned and the towers dismantled in 1920, but the concrete foundations remain as part of an exhibit maintained by the Cape Cod National Seashore.

2. Entering North Truro from the East Along the State Road. The view, ca. 1900, taken from a rise just beyond the Christian Union Church, extends to the left at the junction of Highland Road. At the center, fronting the road, was the grocery store of John G. Thompson, a native of Truro who had followed the sea until, in 1866, at the age of 29, he purchased the business from Sylvanus Hughes. Opposite the store was Mr. Thompson's large grain-and-flour warehouse and his livery stable, erected shortly before 1890. At that time he was reported to have the largest trade in town, and he was undoubtedly prospering, as he also had extensive interests in fish weirs and owned the icehouse at the pond. Mr. Thompson ran the store until his death in about 1920.

3

3. Pond Village. Aside from the fact that the roads are now hard-topped, Pond Village, North Truro (one of the four villages comprising the town of Truro), has changed very little from the day this photograph was taken, ca. 1900. Tradition has it that Miles Standish and his exploring party spent a night along the shore of the pond, where a bronze tablet now commemorates the occasion. At times during the seventeenth and eighteenth centuries, the pond was open to the bay. Attempts were made in 1806 to dig a channel for shipping, but sand repeatedly blocked the entrance and the pond reverted to its present freshwater condition. On the left side of the pond is John G. Thompson's icehouse and loading ramp. The icehouse was transformed into an art school many years ago. The photograph was taken from the railroad station, which stood on the embankment built by the New York, New Haven & Hartford Railroad in the early 1870s. It looks along what was known as Main Street (from the depot to the post office) but is now called Pond Road, from the present intersection of Route 6A to the bay. The road to the right, at the fork toward the bay, just beyond the icehouse, was called Railroad Avenue (now Bayview

Road). In 1893 the only freezer in Truro, the Pond Village Cold Storage, with a capacity of 3000 barrels, was erected on railroad land adjacent to the station. Destroyed by fire in September 1914, it was rebuilt in 1915, with double the original capacity, on low land south of the old site. Unoccupied for a number of years, the building was declared a hazard and leveled in the 1970s.

4. North Truro from the South. "[It] has a neat and thrifty appearance," said the editors of *The History of Barnstable County* in 1890. The area was settled in the early nineteenth century after fishing interests became clustered around the pond and a post office was established there. At the turn of the century, the time of this view, Truro's population was 972, down from its 1850 high of 2051. Almost all of the buildings are easily identifiable today. The large barn at the extreme right was the dairy farm of Michael A. and John L. Rich, brothers who also conducted a business selling wood, hay, grain and coal. The property, originally part of Atkins Hughes's extensive holdings in this part of North Truro, had been inherited by Michael Rich's wife Amelia, Hughes's daughter.

4

5

5. The Center of North Truro. The town is seen from a slight rise just off the road coming from Provincetown, ca. 1900. On the right, at the corner of Pond Road and the State Road, stands the North Truro Primary-Grammar School, a two-room building with grades 1–4 on one side and grades 5–9 on the other. Next to it was the home of Edwin P. Worthen, at that time keeper of the Highland Light Station and postmaster from 1873 to 1889. Both the post office and a store were located in this house, which is virtually unchanged today, though the long, low shed at the rear has been torn down. For many years the school has been the home of Fishnet Industries and is now also occupied by an art gallery and law offices. On the left, at the corner of Highland Road and the State Road, is the building owned by Dutra's Market in 1986. In *Truro, Cape Cod, As I Knew It*, Anthony L. Marshall recalls its occupants around the turn of the century as first "a man named [Benjamin] Hatch and later Miss Elizabeth Small, who sold groceries and some dry goods." There was also a store on the northeast corner where Lillian J. Small sold dry goods, drugs and fancy articles, having taken over her father Abram's grocery business in 1881 and having become postmistress in 1889. Just past the turn in the State Road is the steeple of the Christian Union Church, so called because the Methodists and Congregationalists united and formed one congregation in order to build it in 1840.

6. Highland Light. Seen here in a photograph taken prior to 1901, Highland Light stands on a great bed of gray-blue clay, called the Truro Clay Pounds, in the gully that cuts back into the cliff just north and east

of the light. The clay, which surfaces at various levels across the Cape, ranges in depth from three to 50 feet. No explanation for the term "pounds" has yet been found.

Officially called Cape Cod Light, Highland Light is the fourth most powerful lighthouse in the United States. It was already a popular tourist attraction in the 1880s, when the *Cape Cod Item*, an area newspaper, wrote, "The Town of Truro is urged to provide a better road to Highland Light. There are many summer visitors who, when in the vicinity, desire to visit so interesting a locality, which is now reached only with difficulty." First built in 1798 and rebuilt in 1857, it stands 183 feet above the water on the northeast point of Cape Cod in North Truro. Its four-million-candlepower light is visible for 20 miles, and under certain conditions has been seen over twice that distance. It was originally a fixed white light, but new equipment was installed in 1901, when it became a revolving white light that flashes a beam to all points of the compass every five seconds. In 1932 electricity replaced the oil lamps.

7. The Devil's Backbone. A series of steps going down the cliff below Highland Light, probably built around 1901, was known locally as the Devil's Backbone. Erosion at the site has always been extensive. The lighthouse was built in 1797; 50 years later it was moved back 20 feet and in 1875 the bank was described as losing between four and ten feet a year. The original 1796 deed for the land on which the station is located showed a purchase of ten acres. By 1926 only four remained.

6

7

8

9

8. Highland Light from the North. Nearby, in the view of June 1901, stands the U.S. Navy Wireless Station, which gave ships at sea their location, and the marine reporting station, from which, for 60 years, Isaac Morton Small telegraphed the arrival of passing ships to their Boston or New York merchant owners. At the height of the era, Mr. Small recalled reporting in a single day the passage of four six-masted schooners, six five-masters, 11 four-masters, nine three-masters and 14 two-masters.

9. Laundry Day at Highland Light. A house for the keeper and a double house for two assistants were added when the lighthouse was rebuilt in 1857. In *Cape Cod* (1865), Thoreau describes his three-day stay with the lighthouse keeper. At the time of this photograph, before 1901, the light was run by three keepers who stood watches, as on shipboard. Illumination was provided by three circular wicks within one kerosene burner, replacing the earlier two tiers of whale-oil lamps with 12-inch reflectors. Visible here are the curtains used during the day to shield the reflecting lenses from the sun's rays. In the *Advocate* of May 1875, correspondent Isaac Morton Small reported: "The Highland Lighthouse has received its annual dressing of coal-tar paint and whitewash and we do not remember of ever having seen it look better." A sign at the extreme left advertises souvenirs for sale at Highland House.

10. Highland Light. At the base of the cliff below the light some summer visitors, shielded from the sun by umbrellas, sit at the water's edge, watching the passing ships, ca. 1901.

10

11. The Highland House and Millstone Cottage, North Truro. The James Small family began taking summer boarders at the Highland House, originally a farmhouse, in 1862, when they charged $5 a week for room and board. In 1873 Isaac Morton Small succeeded his father; by 1901 his son Willard was listed as proprietor. The family also maintained golf links, a bowling alley and a livery stable; the barns and a carriage are at right. The *Cape Cod Item* of June 1883 noted: "B. Paine is at work on a skating rink at the Highlands for I. M. Small," and as late as 1920 it observed that there were "one hundred guests at Highland House."

12. Millstone Cottage, Highland House Grounds. Summer boarders play croquet in June 1901. The cottage was built near the site of an early windmill, from which grinding stones were taken and used as entrance steps. (The mill itself still existed as late as 1890, though as a "dismantled wreck" used as an ocean lookout.) According to proprietor Isaac Morton Small, the miller received a peck for each bushel of grain ground at the mill. When this area became part of the Cape Cod National Seashore in the 1960s, the Highland House ceased operation and the Millstone Cottage was offered by the National Park Service to the Truro Historical Society for temporary use as a museum. The building was later moved to a site on the west side of Pond Road, and the Historical Society was given use of the Highland House, where their collection is now on view to the public during the summer season.

13

14

15

13. The Isaac Morton Small Family Domain. A view ca. 1900 shows Highland House, the Millstone Cottage and other buildings.

14. Two Cottages at the Highlands. These were the first two of six cottages added by Mr. Small to the Highland House property between 1900 and 1915. All were known by individual names. These two are identified on a postcard published by Mr. Small, ca. 1901, as the "Rock" (closest in the foreground) and the "Beacon." Rooms were rented in each cottage and board was available at the main house.

15. Corn Hill and the Entrance to Pamet Harbor at the Mouth of the Pamet River. The area was named by the Pilgrims when they discovered some Indian burial sites containing corn; the name Pamet derives from the Indian tribe they found there. When the Pilgrims arrived and explored the area, the shallow harbor was suitable only for very small craft and has remained so despite attempts over the years to dredge it. Nevertheless, for the first half of the nineteenth century, the area prospered with boat-building and its associated crafts, fish packing and stores of all kinds. A lighthouse built there in 1849 was abandoned in 1855, by which time most of the other activities had also ceased or moved away.

On the bluff at Corn Hill stood the six Corn Hill Beach cottages, built in 1898 by Charles W. Snow for Lorenzo Dow Baker of Wellfleet, who owned the land, and the five additional cottages and a larger building called the "Governor Bradford Lodge," added in 1902, the approximate date of this view. A stairway provided access to the beach. In his reminiscences of Truro life at the turn of the century, Anthony L. Marshall describes the cottages as having two or three rooms on the first floor, outside privies and a single cold-water tap in each cottage. Meals, taken at the lodge, were supplied by a concessionaire. This practice, says Mr. Marshall, was discontinued in 1913 when kitchens were added to the individual cottages. A windmill at the top of the hill pumped water into two wooden tanks located to the right of the cottages. Though located far from town, Corn Hill vacationers could pick up the train at the Corn Hill flag station for excursions into Provincetown or up the Cape. Several of the original cottages and the lodge survive today, surrounded by the substantial summer and year-round houses which are continually being added to the landscape.

16. The Road into Provincetown Near Mayflower Heights. The original road, known as the King's Highway, followed over the dunes behind East Harbor (Pilgrim Lake) and entered the town around Snail Road. The pilings visible along the shore are remains of the many windmills used to pump seawater for making salt. The manufacture of salt by solar evaporation began around 1800, was at its height in 1835 and had virtually ceased by 1854, when this road along the beach was laid out. In the harbor in this view of ca. 1900 are Isaac (Ike) Lewis's weirs and wharf. The Boston and Cape Cod Marine Telegraph Co. brought its lines to Provincetown in 1856 and telephone service to the Cape tip began in 1883. In 1920, describing a "Provincetown Pilgrimage" in the magazine *Photo-Era*, Raymond E. Hansen and Herbert B. Turner commented, "The town is pervaded with a strong atmosphere of antiquity. . . . However, it is somewhat marred by a too liberal sprinkling of telephone poles . . ."—an observation that is still perfectly valid!

17. "Cottages and Town from Mr. Horne's." This photograph of ca. 1900 looks along Commercial Street at the far East End. Most of the "cottages" in photographer Snow's title appear to be closed for the season, but the lineup along the waterfront already foretold the 1912 prediction in *New England Magazine*: "The 'Summer business' is an important source of income to Provincetown and one that bids fair to grow to much larger proportions." Mr. Horne was probably Durbin Horne, listed in the 1901 directory as a dry-goods dealer from Pittsburgh who summered in the East End.

Arriving by Boat

19

18. The Steamer *Cape Cod*. Most people came to Provincetown by boat. Here a large holiday crowd awaits the boat, arriving from Boston for Fourth of July festivities. Steamers first began regular runs between Boston and Provincetown in 1842, though they were not excursion boats. Bowley's Wharf, erected in 1849, became Steamboat Wharf in 1863, when it was extended to deep water to accommodate the steamer *George Shattuck*, which continued in service until 1874. In 1883 the *Longfellow* was built expressly for the run, being replaced by the *Cape Cod* in 1902, the year this photograph was taken.

19. Passengers Disembark from the *Cape Cod*. With suitcases and packages, visitors stream down Railroad Wharf into town. The horse-drawn "accommodation" which met all arriving excursion vessels also returned to town. A few years earlier, Brooks Livery Stable advertised "Barges *Empress* and *Myrtle* will be waiting on the arrival of all trains and steamers to convey passengers to the hotels and about town." ("Barge" was a New England term for a large four-wheeled coach with two or more seats.)

20. A View from Railroad Wharf. The schooner to the west of the wharf, seen here ca. 1900, is the *M. L. Wetherell* of Boston. Clearly visible at the head of the wharf is the sign of the New York Store, purveyors of dry goods and clothing until the 1970s. Just to the right of the ship's mast, on the east side of the wharf, is the mansard roof of the public library, erected in 1873 by Nathaniel Freeman and donated to the town. The library occupied the first floor, with the local G.A.R. Post, Women's Relief Corps and other beneficent organizations using the second-floor rooms for their meetings. From 1800 to 1883 the third floor was the studio of photographers Nickerson & Smith (George H. Nickerson and William H. Smith), who advertised "Portraits in all styles" and "Always on hand a large assortment of stereoscopic views of Provincetown."

21. Looking West Alongshore from Railroad Wharf. In 1901, about two years after this photograph was taken, there were 26 stores listed selling groceries and provisions in Provincetown. Perhaps there were additional ones that did not advertise; none of the addresses correspond to the two markets seen here to the east of the Kendrick & Atkins Livery Stable. William R. Kendrick, a former employee of the Samuel Knowles livery stable, and Frank K. Atkins probably started their business around 1893, when Mr. Knowles died and his stable was taken over by the Campbell family.

22. The Railroad Crossing, Standish and Commercial Streets. At the corner of Standish Street the tracks of the Old Colony Railroad (later the New York, New Haven & Hartford) crossed Commercial Street onto Railroad Wharf. With the completion of the last stretch of railroad from Wellfleet in 1873, the 120-mile trip from Boston to Provincetown became the longest run on the Old Colony line. Two trains ran daily in each direction, the trip taking four hours and ten minutes. In addition, there were many special summer excursions to Provincetown and various amenities, such as Pullman parlor-car service on the 4:15 from Boston. The tracks in this section of town were removed in the late 1920s; all passenger service from Boston was discontinued in the late 1940s.

On the left, at 301 Commercial Street, is the store and dwelling of Aylmer F. Small, merchant tailor, dealer in gents' furnishings, foreign and domestic woolens and trimmings. The striped barber pole belonged to John W. Myrick, who rented his building from Mr. Small. At the right-hand corner building, formerly a post office, a sign points to the pool room run by Joseph S. Fisher. Small signs farther down Commercial Street in this 1902 view mark the locations of Zelotes Smith's bakery (at 306) and Mrs. T. L. Chapman's dining rooms across from the library. In the foreground, coming from Railroad Wharf, is one of Provincetown's horse-drawn "jiggers," a flat cart with large wheels used for hauling. The name may have derived from the nautical term jigger, the lowest sail on a jiggermast, or possibly from the jolting movement of the cart. This area is still generally referred to by everyone in Provincetown as "the center of town" and is the dividing point between the East and West Ends.

23. The Pilgrim House, 313 Commercial Street. At the turn of the century Provincetown had four hotels. This one sometimes billed itself as "Ye Olde Pilgrim's Hostelrie" and offered "every convenience and comfort to Tourists, Business Men and Families." Records indicate that it has been run as a hotel since about 1810. It was extensively altered and improved in 1847 and at the time of this photograph, ca. 1898, was leased and operated by Samuel Sands Smith, known as "Uncle Sam." By 1901 it had a new proprietor, W. H. Potter, who offered rooms at $2 per day, special weekly rates for summer guests and a large, cool dining room seating 60. Though the main building looks much the same today, its primary use in recent years has been as a nightclub. The lawn and pergola have been replaced by an outdoor café.

24. The Atlantic House, Masonic Place. This establishment advertised itself as having a quiet, shady location and moderate charges. The white-coated gentleman on the porch in this photograph of ca. 1899 is believed to be Francis (Frank) P. Smith, the proprietor, about whom the local newspaper editorialized in 1873:

> Mr. Smith is constantly adding to the list of his friends by his courteous and accommodating manners and unremitting attention to the wants of his guests. The house is kept scrupulously clean and nice. The furniture and bedding are only one year in service and are clean, fresh and nice. . . . Mr. Smith is an accomplished cook and attends to that dept. personally—consequently his table is a little ahead of common hotel tables and cannot fail to please the most delicate palate.

Born in the Azores in 1835, Frank Smith came to Provincetown in 1851 and followed the sea as a steward for 20 years, when he took over the hotel formerly known as the Union House. The Atlantic House still accepts guests, but is more renowned today for its bars, one of which occupies an addition to the original building located in the open space between the two buildings in this view.

25

25. New Central House. In the late 1880s, The Central House advertised itself as the "only Hotel in Provincetown situated on the beach." Originally known as Ocean Hall and used as a public hall for shows and entertainment, the building was purchased in 1868 by Allen Reed, who enlarged it and converted it into a hotel. Following his death in 1881, Mr. Reed's son James, who also served as deputy inspector and collector of customs, took over as manager. Prior to buying The Central House, the elder Mr. Reed ran the Pilgrim House from 1863 to 1868.

In 1903, the date of this view, the hotel, its covered porch extended around the east side of the building, had become "The New Central House." It offered accommodations for about 75 guests, a billiard and pool room, a ladies' parlor and sitting room and a gents' reading and smoking room. As a result of dredging in the harbor several years

ago, the building, now known as the Crown and Anchor Inn, is surrounded by a considerably deeper sand beach and bathers would now find it difficult, even at high tide, to swim at the base of the building.

26. The *Dorothy Bradford*. This boat, larger and faster than the *Cape Cod* (making the trip in about four hours), began bringing visitors to the Cape tip in 1910. She had staterooms and a bar and boasted a dance floor and, reputedly, a ragtime band. On July 6, 1920 the *Cape Cod Item and Bee* reported: "There were 1,275 passengers on *Dorothy Bradford* Sunday." These figures remained fairly constant on busy weekends through the late 1950s, but after completion of the Mid-Cape Highway made driving from Boston a two-and-a-quarter-hour trip, the number of passengers declined. Now 600 is considered a top day.

The Monument

27. The Monument. As early as 1852 proposals had been made for a memorial to celebrate the first landing of the Pilgrims at Provincetown and the historic signing of the Mayflower Compact in Provincetown Harbor, but it was more than 50 years before the project was realized. The completed Monument rises 252 feet seven-and-a-half inches from the ground and 352 feet over the Provincetown waterfront. The original proposal was for "plain, rough stone, just as high as possible, which could be seen from every town on Cape Cod and from every vessel, in any reasonably fair weather, coming in or going out of Massachusetts Bay." In a public competition more than 100 designs were offered and it was finally decided to adopt the form of a campanile or bell tower. When no suitable English or Dutch tower could be found, the Torre del Mangia in Siena was copied.

28. Work Begins on the Monument. The southeast cornerstone block of North Carolina granite, weighing 4800 pounds, is lowered into place. Reinforcing rods of twisted steel rise from the eight-foot-deep foundation of solid concrete. The large crowd at the 1907 ceremony listened to speeches by politicians including the Governor of Massachusetts and the President of the United States, and surely were to be forgiven if their attention wandered during Teddy Roosevelt's 4000-word lecture advocating a federal law governing companies engaged in interstate commerce and strict enforcement of the Sherman antitrust laws. This divergence from the matter at hand is probably no stranger than some of the 29 items placed in a copper box buried in the cornerstone. They range from a predictable list of contributors to the Monument-building fund to a copy of Massachusetts Governor Curtis Guild's Memorial Day speech delivered at New York University's Hall of Fame to the Seventh Annual Report of the United Fruit Company (Lorenzo Dow Baker of nearby Wellfleet, founder of the company, had contributed $1000 to the Monument Fund).

29. Laying the Blocks. In June 1908 workmen from the Milton, Massachusetts firm of Maguire & O'Hearn, whose low bid of $73,865 had secured them the contract, began the task of laying the granite blocks quarried in Stonington, Maine. They were given until the end of 1909 to finish the job or incur a $5 per day penalty.

To the West'ard

30. Looking West from Just above Freeman Street. This photograph was taken from the Center Methodist Church steeple in 1899. Provincetown had already reached its 1885 peak of 4480 inhabitants and was the most populous town on Cape Cod. Still, the *Boston Traveler* would advise in its columns, "No better place exists in which to spend a lazy, quiet vacation."

31. The Samuel Knowles Livery Stable. Melting snow covers the empty lot across the street from the stable in this photograph of ca. 1890 by photographer George H. Nickerson, some of whose negatives were in Louis Snow's collection. Born in Truro in 1831, Mr. Knowles served from 1862 to 1863 in the 23rd Massachusetts Volunteers. He was discharged from the 33rd Regiment, Massachusetts Infantry for disability and in 1864 bought a grocery store in North Truro. He ran this business for only a year, selling it in 1865 and purchasing the stage-coach-and-mail route between Orleans and Provincetown. (The stage, with its roll-up leather curtains, is to the left of the stable.) In 1873, Knowles established a livery stable and grain store at 276 Commercial Street, advertising "careful drivers," as well as offering flour, meal, grain, feed and hay for sale. The door to the left of the stable's main entrance led to the office of the N.Y. & Boston Despatch Express Co., for which Mr. Knowles was the agent. In the late 1880s his ads advised families they could procure fresh produce by train from Boston by using the express company's services. Mr. Knowles died in 1893 and his express and livery business was taken over by the Campbell family. Not much appears in the records about Jesse Rogers, house carpenter. He is listed in the 1886 directory as carpenter and builder, living at Prince Street near the church, as is his son, Jesse, Jr. In the 1901 directory he has moved both his business and home to Lancy's Corner, Commercial Street; no further mention is made of his son.

32. Store, ca. 1890. The location of this George H. Nickerson view has not been identified. The signs advertise beer on ice, cigars and tobacco. On display outside the shop are what appear to be baskets of blueberries, grapes, bananas, apples and tomatoes. The black dog has just come from a swim. On the building next door is the intriguing sign "It Floats."

31

32

33

34

33. Town Hall. This view was taken ca. 1905 from an upstairs window in one of the houses across Commercial Street prior to the widening of Ryder Street in 1920. On the lawn are a watering trough and a tablet commemorating the signing of the Mayflower Compact.

Provincetown's first town hall, destroyed by fire on February 16, 1877, had been built in 1853 on High Pole Hill on the site of the present Pilgrim Monument. Prior to that time, church buildings had been used for town business. The present Town Hall was erected in 1880 at a cost of $50,400. The old Ryder homestead land was donated for the site and the clock and bell were also given by prominent citizens. Among the hall's accoutrements described in accounts of the opening were "tables, dishes and necessary appliances in the basement for setting up a collation or supper" and in the auditorium a large stage with a "fine and full set of scenery" which cost over $1000. A rare broadside of the time advertised "First Entertainment in the New Town Hall Aug. 30. Illustrated tour of Europe with stereopticon by Sidney Dickinson, A.M. will furnish the citizens of Provincetown an unequalled opportunity to see the fitness of their new and superb hall for the highest class of amusements."

To the left of Town Hall stood the Congregational Church, also called Church of the Pilgrims. Built in 1843, it incorporated portions taken from the frame of the old White Oak Meeting House, so called because locally cut white oak had been used. That building, dating from 1792, was the third church built in Provincetown and stood on the site now occupied by the Catholic Church. In 1873 the Congregational Church was renovated. A brick basement was installed to house one large and two smaller vestries. It was rededicated on February 20, 1874, just 100 years after the dedication of the original White Oak Church. The building has not been used as a church for many years; most recently it was run as a movie house, the long area in front serving as an outdoor café.

34. The East Side and Back of Town Hall, Seen from Town Hill. The large white house with gingerbread trim in this 1905 view now stands on the corner of Bradford and Ryder Streets, all the houses to the west of it having been removed when Ryder Street was widened and a park created at the base of Monument Hill. Five buildings, housing stores and dwellings, were removed between Town Hall and the Seaman's Savings Bank (directly behind the white house), including the house

on Bradford Street opposite the Town Hall. The project had been bitterly opposed by those directly affected, as well as by many others, but "progress" prevailed. Using funds contributed jointly by the federal, state and town governments, a park was constructed, at the rear of which is the bronze bas-relief depicting the signing of the Mayflower Compact in the cabin of the *Mayflower* while she lay at anchor in Provincetown Harbor. One tragic result of the project was the suicide of Joshua "Tom" Small, longtime proprietor of the bakery at Gosnold and Commercial Streets. Mr. Small's house, the former Rebecca Hilliard property at the corner of Ryder and Commercial Streets, was one of those taken for the widening. He became so despondent after its destruction that he went to the area of the bas-relief and shot himself, succumbing to the gunshot wound on August 9, 1921, at the age of 68 years.

35. Looking Southwest from Town Hill. The spire of the Universalist Church rises above the large white building belonging to the Odd Fellows at the corner of Bradford and Winslow Streets. The lodge hall, built in 1832 by a share company and called the Village Hall, was used for meetings, dances and social gatherings. When it was purchased by the Odd Fellows in 1846, the upper floor was fitted out as meeting rooms. In 1890 the Marine Lodge No. 96 had about 220 members and was the largest such organization in Provincetown. The Universalist Church, built in 1847 after a design by Christopher Wren, is noted for the beautiful trompe-l'œil inside the building, which has been extensively restored to near-original condition in recent years.

36. Looking East from Town Hill. In this view, ca. 1899, Campbell's livery stable can be seen on Commercial Street, a short distance from Ryder Street, at the extreme right.

37

37. The Area Around Gosnold and Commercial Streets. The mortar and pestle sign hangs outside of Adams' Pharmacy, which also advertises "ice cold sodas all flavors" in this pre-1899 view. Clearly visible on the left is the plank sidewalk begun in 1838 with the town's share of the revenue distributed by the state during Andrew Jackson's administration, and the oil-burning street lamps, installed in 1884 and converted to electricity 20 years later. The bakery sign hangs on the building at 244 Commercial Street, which housed Joshua T. Small's bakery and, upstairs, the meeting rooms of the Nautilus Club, a ladies' group that still exists. Mr. Small, who had succeeded N. H. Drie as baker in 1878, purchased this location from Jacob Gross in 1882. By 1886 he advertised that he sold not only "fresh pies, cakes and breads," but also "Coming flour" which contains more gluten than any other, as well as paper, bags and twine. In June 1883, the *Cape Cod Item*, a regional newspaper published in Yarmouthport, commented in their Provincetown column: "Some of the nicest pieces of artistic work that have been done in this place were the cakes that were got up for the graduating class supper by J. T. Small. The class cake with monogram and several members' cakes with mottoes and initials were really fine pieces of work. There is no need of going out of town for wedding or fair cakes as he furnishes these articles at less than Boston prices."

38. Commercial and Carver Streets. The Gifford House banner flies over Commercial Street at the corner of Carver Street, where a sign points the way to the hotel. Opened in 1868, Gifford's Summer Hotel advertised a "Bath House attached to the premises," and was the post stop for the Boston stage. It was host to Presidents Taft and Roosevelt during the festivities connected with the building of the Monument. Its proprietor, James Gifford, also served the town as

collector of customs. Just below the Gifford House banner on the left, a pool sign indicates the location of Charles L. Hudson's pool rooms at 201 Commercial Street. Photographer Snow's title for this photograph is "Opposite John Adams Market." The market, to the right of the banner, was built in 1865. Mr. Adams purchased it in 1884 and remodeled it to accommodate a large refrigerator or cooling-room for meats and installed a railway to facilitate its handling. It was the largest store of its kind in town. Mr. Adams' ads also offered "free prompt delivery to any part of the village" of groceries, flour, country produce, beef, poultry, mutton, lamb, veal, pork, bacon, tongue and canned goods.

39. Commercial Street in the Area of Court Street. The flagpole stands outside of the fire station at the corner of Court Street. To the west, at the head of Steamboat Wharf, purchased by their father, William Matheson, in 1882, is the shop of Mary and Jessie Matheson. The building had been constructed in 1851 by Joshua and Gideon Bowley as a general outfitting store for ships. It was remodeled by Mr. Matheson, the front being set up for his daughters, the rear containing the office from which he managed his fleet of vessels engaged in the Grand Banks and West India Trade. East of the firehouse, on the establishment of William T. Bangs at 190 Commercial Street, a sign advertises "Magee Ranges." Mr. Bangs dealt in stoves, tinware and plumbing and also sold and repaired bicycles. Opposite the Mathesons' was E. J. Kilburn's, dealer in foreign and domestic fruit, pure confectionery, fancy goods, periodicals, etc., and the grocery operated at 175 Commercial Street by Manual Rogers. Commercial Street remains 22 feet wide today, though it no longer accommodates two-way auto traffic, an arrangement that continued until the late 1930s.

40. View from Manta's Wharf, 180 Commercial Street. The brig *D. A. Small* is tied up to Dyer's Wharf in a view of ca. 1899 encompassing an area about one-half block east and west of Winthrop Street. Coming to the United States in 1854, Joseph Manta followed the sea until 1876, when he started a grocery store nearly west of the wharf bearing his name, which he purchased in 1882. Manta soon became extensively involved in the wholesale fishing business, acting as agent for several large schooners engaged in the fresh fish business. He was also listed in Provincetown's 1886 directory as a "fish maker," meaning he prepared dried salt cod. Neither his wharf nor Dyer's still exist, but the large white building across the street from the Centenary Methodist Church is still run as Dyer's Hardware Store.

41. The Centenary Methodist Church. At the corner of Commercial and Winthrop Streets stood the Centenary Methodist Church, seen in a photograph taken ca. 1900 from across Commercial Street in a room above Dyer's Hardware. Built in 1866, after Methodists living in the West End decided they wanted a place of worship closer to their residences, the church cost $40,000 and had an auditorium with a capacity of over 1000. The steeple, crowned by a large gilded ball and rising 165 feet, was guaranteed to be at least one foot higher than that of the mother church, the Center Methodist Church.

42. Ruins of the Centenary Methodist Church. The structure was destroyed by fire on Saturday, March 14, 1908, after a bolt of lightning struck the spire in the early hours of the morning, during a brief but violent thunderstorm. For two hours the fire burned feebly and appeared to be confined to the steeple. Although jets from the fire hoses were unable to reach the flames, the only concern was of flooding the magnificent pipe organ in the choir loft. None of the church furnishings was removed except the big desk Bible. Suddenly, the fire leaped uncontrollably outward from between the walls and from the coal bins in the basement. The heat became so intense that nearby roofs, still wet from the rain, began to burn and clouds of steam rose from buildings as far removed as the Fisherman's Cold Storage, several blocks away. By 5 A.M. the great church was reduced to a heap of charred wood. A second church built on the same site was purchased in 1948 and later razed by the First National Bank of Provincetown, which occupies the building there today. Most of the surrounding houses, though often altered, still stand.

41

42

35

43. The Red Inn. "Cottages and Creek west from Gull Hill," was Mr. Snow's identification of this photograph of ca. 1899. The house is the Red Inn, for years a fashionable summer lodge, run by Miss Charlotte Wilson, that remains a very popular restaurant. In 1922, in *The Provincetown Book*, Nancy Paine Smith said,"Mill Creek at the West End is filling rapidly now that the breakwater [built by the government in 1911] shuts it off from the harbor. . . . Fresh Water Mill Pond and Salt Water Mill Pond fed by the Mill Creek have entirely disappeared. . . ."

In the East End

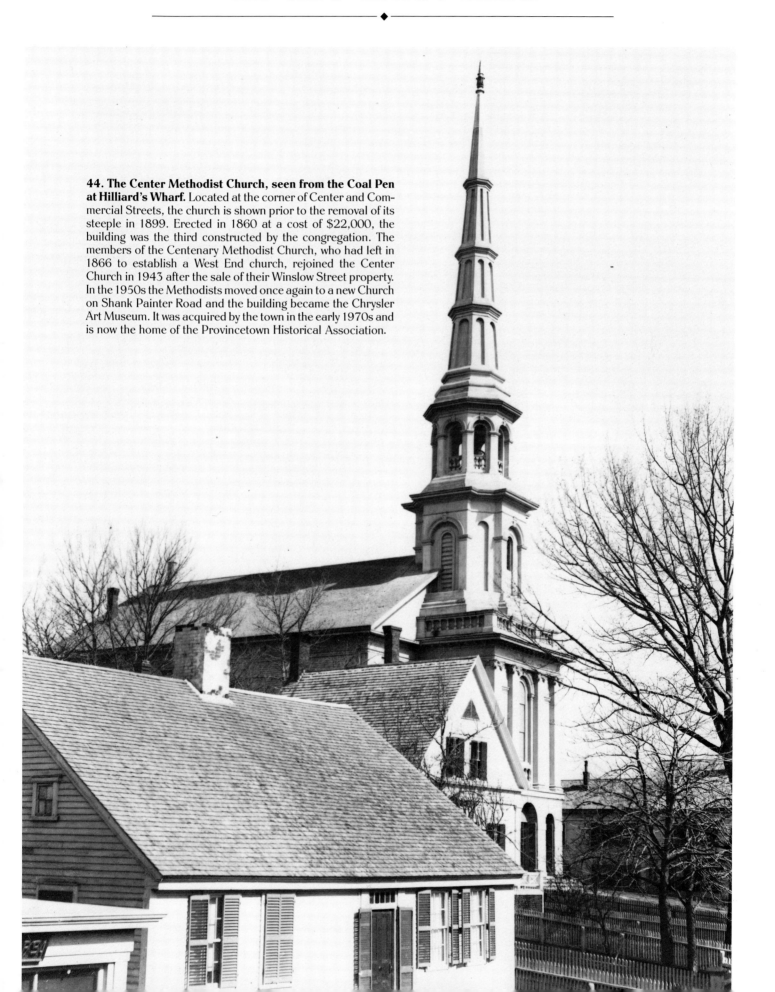

44. The Center Methodist Church, seen from the Coal Pen at Hilliard's Wharf. Located at the corner of Center and Commercial Streets, the church is shown prior to the removal of its steeple in 1899. Erected in 1860 at a cost of $22,000, the building was the third constructed by the congregation. The members of the Centenary Methodist Church, who had left in 1866 to establish a West End church, rejoined the Center Church in 1943 after the sale of their Winslow Street property. In the 1950s the Methodists moved once again to a new Church on Shank Painter Road and the building became the Chrysler Art Museum. It was acquired by the town in the early 1970s and is now the home of the Provincetown Historical Association.

45

45. Northwest from the Center Methodist Church Steeple. This view of 1899 overlooks the area around Standish and Bradford Streets and Town Hill, now the site of the Pilgrim Monument. The building at the center with a tower, the Center School, was torn down and is now a parking lot. Nearby is the railroad station. The house with a mansard roof on the extreme right is now a shop. The undeveloped area between them was the site of Duarte's Garage, now closed. Behind the railroad station is the sign of Bennett's Ice.

Stephen Bennett came to Provincetown in 1842 at the age of 18 and worked as a ship rigger for several years. In 1870 he began his ice business by cutting and storing 40 tons of pond ice, building himself an icehouse and stable. As fish weirs began to be installed and the fresh-fish business grew, the demand for ice increased, and by 1890 Mr. Bennett owned several ponds and had facilities for storing 5000 tons of ice. Only three days was needed for cutting that quantity of ice, during which time he employed 110–120 men and nine horses at a cost of about $1000. During the rest of the year he had six men

constantly delivering ice. He himself handled the hotel and family trade "with a fine span of coal black horses." In the 20 years after he began there were three years when the ponds did not freeze sufficiently to cut a single pound of ice.

The long white building near the upper-right corner of the photograph is the almshouse on Alden Street, constructed in 1870 at a cost of $6526. It replaced a building of 1833 and was described as "affording a comfortable and commodious home for the unfortunate dependents upon the town's charity." In recent years it has served as a town-operated nursing home and, since the construction of a new facility, houses several town offices.

46. Looking North from the Center Methodist Church Steeple. This view, taken in 1899, includes the cemetery. The road on the left is Center Street, which crosses Bradford Street just beyond the second house. A short stretch of Johnson Street is visible on the extreme right. The long dark building behind the water tower was the railroad freight house on Standish Avenue.

47. View from the Steeple of the Center Methodist Church, Looking East from Johnson Street, 1899.

48. Provincetown Cold Storage. A view from the steeple of the Center Methodist Church, taken in 1899 at low tide, overlooks the Provincetown Cold Storage at the foot of Johnson Street. All of the white buildings in the foreground were part of the freezer plant facilities, the first to be constructed in Provincetown, in 1893. The trolley that brought fish from the trap boats directly into the plant is at the extreme right. Of the six cold-storage structures once located in Provincetown, only one still stands today, the former Consolidated Cold Storage opposite Howland Street; its use is now residential.

51

49. The *Nile*. Out of Portland, Maine, the ship lies at anchor off Hilliard's Wharf prior to 1899. To the east of the Center Methodist Church are the "water" and "ice" signs of the Province-town Cold Storage buildings at the foot of Johnson Street. Hilliard's Wharf was run by John D. Hilliard, who in 1880 took over a wholesale fish business and general store begun nearly 50 years earlier by his grandfather Thomas and other family members.

50. The Center Methodist Church. This photograph dates from ca. 1900, after the removal of the church's steeple, which had stood 162 feet above the ground. It was taken down by Irving Freeman, a local contractor and builder, after it had been struck by lightning. The view encompasses the area from about Johnson Street at the right to Hilliard's Wharf (presently Lands End Marine) at the left. On the 1882 panoramic map of Provincetown, Center Street is called Church Street.

51. The Waterfront from D. A. Small's Wharf. The view looks east, a block or two past Pearl Street. Wooden dories, seen in the foreground, have become virtually nonexistent.

52. Children at Play. Along the shore, probably the area east from near Dyer Street, youngsters play in a dory and a sailing dory. "Our boys cannot remember when they learned to swim and to handle a boat," writes Nancy Paine Smith in *The Provincetown Book*.

53. Along Commercial Street, Near Kendall Lane. The white house on the left is the Kendall Cottage; the Mayo Cottage is visible next door through the trees. The Surfside Arms Motel now occupies the entire site on both sides of the street in the foreground of the photograph.

53

54. The Mayo Cottage, 493 Commercial Street. 55. The Kendall Cottage, 495 Commercial Street. The cottages, the homes of Captain Edwin C. Mayo, mariner, and Jesse I. Kendall, stood next door to each other. In 1890 the Mayo home was listed as "Seaside Cottage for summer visitors only," but the 1901 Provincetown directory refers to it as Mayo's Cottage. In that year Mrs. Marietta G. Small was listed as the owner of the Kendall home. In more recent times the two properties were combined and operated as the Seascape House. They were torn down in the 1960s to make way for the present Surfside Arms Motel, now 543 Commercial Street.

56. A Summer Day on the Beach. The view, taken at the foot of Kendall Lane, ca. 1898, looks towards Philip Whorf's Wharf at 489 Commercial Street. The house at the right, number 491, which belonged to Lysander D. Mayo, a fish maker, is still standing. All the other buildings have been torn down.

57. Looking West at Low Tide. Charles Nordhoff wrote in *Harper's* some years before this view of ca. 1900 was taken: "at low water, you may see a good many articles of last year's wear and use, and smell the seemingly immortal odors of some of last year's fish, revealed by the departing tide."

58. Mt. Pleasant House. Following the completion of the last stretch of railroad from Wellfleet to Provincetown in 1873, many more summer visitors began arriving in Provincetown, and more lodgings were needed for them. The Mt. Pleasant House on Bradford Street in the East End stands virtually unchanged today from this photograph of ca. 1900, when it was listed as a hotel run by proprietor Mrs. Mary Days. Bradford Street, the second of Provincetown's two streets running east–west, was earlier known as Parallel Street. It was completed at a cost of $29,000 and opened to travel in the same year as the railroad, when the town's continuing growth made it a necessity. In the 20 years after 1855, Provincetown's population had increased by more than a thousand people from 3096 to 4537.

The Photographer and His Surroundings

59. The Amphion Orchestra. Photographer Louis Snow is at the extreme right, as violinist with the orchestra, ca. 1900. The group hired the Town Hall auditorium for dances every Friday night for many years, charging admission fees of 50¢ for gentlemen, 15¢ for ladies and 15¢ to sit in the balcony and watch. According to Mr. Snow's son Stanley, the group made an incredible $400 per member for the event they ran during the 1907 festivities accompanying the dedication of the Provincetown Monument. The orchestra also traveled to play at dances in Truro (a two-hour wagon trip each way in those days). Other members of the group identified are: Sarah Johnson, pianist and local music teacher; her husband George, a mason, on bass; Frank Chase, seated second from left, cornet player. The Johnsons resided on Masonic Place. Mr. Chase worked at Paine's Wharf and lived at 113 Commercial Street. The remaining members of the orchestra came from Boston on the steamer every week.

60

60. The Snow House, 6 Washington Avenue. "Our house from Capt. Curran's," was Louis Snow's title for this ca. 1900 view of the family home, photographed from the house of Captain William Curran at 343 Commercial Street. Three generations of the Snow family lived in the house at this time: Louis, his father Olin and grandfather Obadiah. The house, in 1986 owned by the Salvador Vasques family, had been built about 1850 by Louis Morris, Olin's maternal grandfather, who was lost at sea on a voyage to the West Indies.

61. The Snow Sitting Room. The room, seen ca. 1900, looks into the parlor. Stanley Snow, photographer Louis' son, believes the portrait on the wall to the right of the curtained entryway to be that of his great-grandfather Obadiah (1825–1906).

62. The Snow Sitting Room. Prominent is the Emerson upright piano which, Stanley Snow recalls, had an attachment for use with piano-player rolls. The Snows, agents for the Emerson Piano Co. at their Commercial Street store, were a musical family. In her chapter on churches and Methodists in *The Provincetown Book*, Nancy P. Smith wrote: "For 60 years Obadiah Snow was a chorister of remarkable ability. With a sweet and true tenor voice, assisted by a leader on each part, and by his son Olin at the piano, when he lifted the baton and said 'Now, Olin,' he made the vestry rock with singing."

63

64

65

63. The Retail Establishment of Obadiah Snow & Son, 250 Commercial Street. The photograph was taken by grandson Louis prior to 1903. The elder Mr. Snow had purchased the house on the right side in 1873 and the one to the east of it two years later—a small house that was jacked up and joined to the other property by the single large store. There he sold music, pianos, fancy goods, carpets and other household furnishings. Displayed in the windows are items ranging from pitcher-and-washbowl sets to carpets and a bicycle.

64. The Enlarged Snow Establishment. About 1903, the Snows enlarged the original building to include three upstairs bedrooms.

More musical instruments, ranging from banjos to saxophones, are featured in the store windows at this time. In later years, Louis Snow lived in the right-hand apartment with his son Stanley and his wife, while his son Morris and his wife lived on the other side. Louis Snow ran the store until about 1925–26, when he sold it.

65. Interior of the Snow Family Store. The merchandise in this view of ca. 1900 includes sleds, doll carriages and toy wagons, glass cruets, picture frames and sentimental lithos in the Victorian taste, chamber pots, kerosene lamps, violins, scatter rugs, Bissell's carpet sweepers and the Crown Porcelain egg separator (ten cents!).

66. The *Judith*. This was the last boat built by Obadiah Snow, being constructed ca. 1898–99. In the 1850 Federal census Obadiah was listed as a boatbuilder. According to his great-grandson Stanley, he worked out of a building on the waterfront where the Preston Hall parking lot is now located. The *Judith*, however, was built in a shed at the rear of the family store. Stanley recalls hearing that the shed was swamped during the destructive Portland Gale of November 26–27, 1898, and it was feared that the boat would be lost. She suffered no damage, was sold shortly after she was built and was delivered to her new owners at East Boston.

67. "East from Store Cupola." The cupola was located on a kitchen ell at the rear of the Snows' store and home at 250 Commercial Street. Several "jiggers" (Provincetown's particular flat hauling wagons) are drawn up to New York, New Haven & Hartford Railroad freight cars and one from the New York, Chicago and St. Louis line on Railroad Wharf. There is some difference of opinion regarding the square wooden pipes in the foreground: Some people believe they were sewer drains, others that they are the remains of pipes used to pump seawater into the salt evaporation pans. Some sewage did drain into the bay (though illegally) as late as the 1960s.

68

69

68. Ice in the Harbor. During periods of prolonged low temperatures, ice forms in Cape Cod Bay and southwest winds bring it into Provincetown Harbor, partially closing the area. A frequently repeated story tells of times when it was possible to walk to Long Point or from Truro to Provincetown on the ice, and though scenes such as this do occur from time to time, it seems unlikely, given the depth of the harbor and the 12-foot tides, that it has ever frozen over completely. Here, during the especially cold winter of 1902, a group of schoolboys poses on the ice with Railroad Wharf in the background.

69. "Icebergs." If freezing occurs in the harbor, "icebergs" up to eight feet thick are left behind on the shore when the tide goes out. It was probably a fairly unusual event even in 1902, when Louis Snow photographed his father Olin (upper right), Lowell Cook (upper left), Captain Matthew William Burt (lower left) and Charlie Cook on the beach at the foot of Gosnold Street. Captain Burt had been master of the last of the Provincetown-to-Boston packets, the *James P. Foster.* Charles Cook ran a ship chandlery at 240 Commercial Street. Sand dredged from the harbor in the 1960s has raised the level of the beach in this area to the top of the pilings seen in the right of the photo.

70. A Class of Charles Webster Hawthorne. "On sunny days the class model would be posed (clothed) . . . seated in the full glare of the sun with her face shaded either by a hat or parasol. . . ." Thus Dorothy Gees Seckler, in her definitive study of the Provincetown art colony, described the early classes of Charles Webster Hawthorne (1872–1930), the painter generally given credit for establishing Provincetown as one of the foremost art colonies in America. Mr. Hawthorne is seen here, dressed impeccably in white flannels, ca. 1900, during one of his weekly demonstration classes, held outdoors in good weather. The son of a sea captain from Maine, Hawthorne had been a teaching assistant to the master painter William Merritt Chase at the National Academy and the Art Students League and at a summer art school run by Mr. Chase at Southampton, New York. After Chase closed the school and sold the property, Hawthorne opened his own Cape Cod School of Painting at Provincetown in 1899, attracted by the town's European look and inexpensive facilities.

70

A Seafaring Town:
Earning a Livelihood...

71

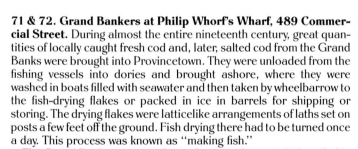

71 & 72. Grand Bankers at Philip Whorf's Wharf, 489 Commercial Street. During almost the entire nineteenth century, great quantities of locally caught fresh cod and, later, salted cod from the Grand Banks were brought into Provincetown. They were unloaded from the fishing vessels into dories and brought ashore, where they were washed in boats filled with seawater and then taken by wheelbarrow to the fish-drying flakes or packed in ice in barrels for shipping or storing. The drying flakes were latticelike arrangements of laths set on posts a few feet off the ground. Fish drying there had to be turned once a day. This process was known as "making fish."

The Grand Bankers seen in these photographs, ca. 1898, sailed in April or May for the Grand Banks off Newfoundland and returned in September. During the Civil War fish prices were very high and crew members earned from \$200–500 per man per trip. By comparison, 1889, when only one vessel returned with a full load of fish, was an extremely poor year. That ship was the schooner *Willie A. McKay*, skippered by Captain Angus McKay, who in 1882 returned with the largest catch of fish ever brought into Provincetown. After being dried and readied for market they weighed 4062 quintals (a metric unit equivalent to 100 kilos) and sold for a little over \$22,000.

73. Finback Whale. This, one of Snow's Nickerson plates, is nearly identical to one in Herman Jennings' 1890 book on Provincetown, in which the creature is identified as one of the largest finbacks ever taken in Provincetown. According to Jennings, it was killed by Joshua S. Nickerson on the whaling schooner *A. B. Nickerson.* It measured 65'4" long, 14'6" across the tail, 11 feet along its lower jaw, length of fins 10 feet, girth 37 feet, and was estimated to weigh 136 tons. Sold to a Chicago syndicate for exhibition, it was taken through the "western country" on a specially constructed flatcar. Captain Newton P. West, a mariner who resided on Webster Place, went along as lecturer.

74

75

60

74. Samuel S. Swift's Wharf Opposite Howland Street. When George H. Nickerson took this photograph ca. 1890, Mr. Swift owned four vessels engaged in the Grand Banks fishery. He also sold prepared fish. At the left is the 137-ton *Willie Swift*, built in 1875 in Provincetown by John G. Whitcomb. The ship closest to the shore on the right is the *Ellen A. Swift*, listed as a whaler in 1893 in *Starbuck's History of American Whale Fishing*. Behind her is a vessel whose name is only partly visible, the *Annie R. K——* (Knowles?). Between the ships' masts can be seen the belfry of the Eastern School, now the site of the American Legion Hall.

75. The *Jessie T. Matheson*. Another of the photographs attributed to Nickerson shows the three-masted schooner *Jessie T. Matheson*, named after the daughter of William Matheson, a Nova Scotian who came to Provincetown in 1848 and prospered. The *Cape Cod Item* of October 5, 1883 reported: ". . . schooner *Jessie T. Matheson* has been painted and repaired and will probably go into West India or South American trade this winter." A similar vessel of 193 tons, named after another daughter, the *Lizzie W. Matheson* was described by Jennings as being one of 41 Grand Bank schooners sailing out of Provincetown in 1890. Captain Matheson owned eight such vessels as well as Steamboat Wharf, from which he conducted a wholesale fish business. Jessie and her sister Mary occupied the building at the head of the wharf at 186 Commercial Street, where they sold "dry and fancy goods, feltings, fancy silks, flosses, chenille, etc."

76. The Brig *D. A. Small* Tied Up to Dyer's Wharf. In the foreground is George T. Standish's spar yard. The work of forming a ship's mast from a huge log with a shipwright's adz and a variety of special planes was done completely by hand, using only the experienced eye as a gauge. The brig appears to be undergoing some repairs. She was constructed and launched in Provincetown by John G. Whitcomb in November 1868. Owned by Captain William Curran of 343 Commercial Street, she was listed by Jennings as one of the last seven whaling vessels still operating in 1890. At the left are Manta's Wharf and, at Matheson's Wharf at Court Street, the *Longfellow*, a 413-ton wooden-hulled steamer that ran between Boston and Provincetown from 1883 until 1903. The following year she went into freight service and was carrying a load of explosives from Wilmington, Delaware to Portsmouth, New Hampshire when she began leaking off Cape Cod. The crew was forced to abandon her about four miles off Highland Light and she sank. The nature of her cargo discouraged salvage attempts and in November 1904, during a November gale, she blew up, her remains littering the beach from Peaked Hill Bars to Eastham.

...And Boating for Pleasure

77. Yachts at Anchor. For many years pleasure boats of the New York Yacht Club called at Provincetown on their way to regattas in Marblehead. Here they are seen at anchor, in a view taken from Town Hill, ca. 1903. Writing in *Harper's Magazine* about a visit to the Cape some years earlier, Charles Nordhoff said: "When the spacious harbor is full of vessels . . . this makes one of the prettiest sights imaginable. It has happened before now that a thousand sail of fishermen dropped anchor in the harbor at once. . . . It is estimated that the harbor can accommodate 3000 ships.".

78

78. The *Melba*. A gaff-rigged catboat owned by postmaster Joseph A. West, the boat is seen ca. 1898. Mr. West came to Provincetown from Nova Scotia in 1848 at the age of two. In 1868, with Josiah F. Brown, he succeeded C. P. Dyer as a dealer in furniture, becoming sole owner of the business the same year. In 1886, his store at 248 Commercial Street advertised everything from bird cages to clothes wringers to cabinetmaker's hardware. He also did upholstering and repairing. Sometime between then and 1901 he apparently sold his business to James Atkins and became postmaster. On the shore at the left is a building with the initials of the Cape Cod Yacht Club, in which nearly all the Cape towns were represented. It sponsored regattas each season at various points around the shore.

79. Launching the *Charlotte*. The launching of the schooner *Charlotte* at John Whitcomb's shipyard at 421 Commercial Street on June 18, 1901, was a gala occasion. Photographer Louis Snow was commissioned to record the event, as he had recorded her entire construction, at the request of the yacht's owner, Chicago millionaire James A. Lawrence. No vessel of this size had been built in Province-

town since about 1875, and schools were let out so that youngsters might witness the launch. So many of Provincetown's residents came, it was reported, that the crush of wagons and carriages created what is probably the town's first documented traffic jam. A log boom was laid to smooth the water and, at the stroke of noon, Mrs. Lawrence smashed the traditional bottle of champagne across the yacht's bow, sending her down the ways into the harbor.

Mr. Whitcomb, a native of Yarmouth, Maine, built his first vessel in Provincetown at the age of 31: the 137-ton whaling schooner *Alcyone*, launched in 1866. Over a ten-year period he built several other large ships, including the 166-ton *D. A. Small*, but after 1875 his yard was occupied solely with repairs, until construction of the pleasure boat began in 1900. The shipyard is now a parking lot.

80. The *Charlotte's* First Voyage. James Lawrence's craft is seen under almost full sail in June 1901. "Retired shipmasters, as well as pleasure seekers own handsome yachts and engage in the sport," commented the editor of the *History of Barnstable County* in 1890.

81. The *James Woolley*. This commercial tugboat, a party of guests aboard, is probably visiting Provincetown on a Sunday outing, ca. 1900. Prior to the opening of the Cape Cod Canal in 1914, tugboats with a string of barges in tow were a common sight in Provincetown Harbor, where they frequently took refuge from stormy weather.

82. The *Ashumet*. The yacht is taking part in the M.Y.R.A. (Massachusetts Yacht Racing Association) events of August 1898. She also was mentioned as visiting Provincetown with the New York Yacht Club in 1903. Visible under the *Ashumet's* main boom is the superstructure of the ram *Katahdin*, a battleship with a heavily reinforced and long bow intended to pierce the hull of another vessel. She was at that time the only capital ship of its kind. (And the last?)

83. The *Nancy*. The fishing sloop, owned by Captain Ed Walter Smith of 5 Law Street, is shown ca. 1898. During the destructive Portland Gale of November that year, the *Nancy* was driven ashore at Plymouth, but suffered no real damage. Luckily she was out of Provincetown during the storm, when many vessels were lost or seriously damaged. Captain Smith remains vivid in the memories of many Provincetown residents today; he was nearly 93 when he died in 1944 and was at one time holder of the *Boston Post* cane, awarded to the town's oldest living resident.

81

The Navy Comes to Call

84. A Visit by Teddy Roosevelt's Great White Fleet. A view from Town Hill, probably taken in 1905, shows the Navy's Atlantic Squadron, a group of warships that conducted summer exercises in and around Provincetown Harbor from the late 1870s until before the First World War. "The spectacle is always an interesting one," wrote Everett Ladd Clarke in *New England Magazine.* "The great ships swinging at anchor or going and coming on their mysterious errands, in response to the unending signals, brilliant at night or sharply outlined against the blue waters by day, hold the attention tirelessly for hours."

85. The U.S.S. *Iowa*. Boats for hire transport sailors ashore from the *Iowa* in July 1905. By 1886 visitors to Provincetown could avail themselves of a chance to sail around the harbor; at Steamboat Wharf four "pleasure yachts" were available to take out passengers. They were the *Arbutus* (Captain John E. Freeman of Tremont Street), the *Echo* (Captain Charles H. Walker of 33 Alden Street), the *Florence* (Captain Thomas Mayo of Carver Street) and the *Henrietta* (Captain Silas Nickerson of Commercial Street).
86. The U.S.S. *Texas*. 87. The U.S.S. *Iowa*. These photographs were taken during the Navy's Atlantic Squadron's 1905 visit for summer exercises in Provincetown Harbor.

85

88

88. Evans Field. Visiting sailors from the U.S.S. *Missouri* and other battleships enjoy a field day at Evans Field, July 4, 1905. Prior to this time men from the Atlantic Fleet taking part in summer exercises in Provincetown Harbor had used Lem Frank Nickerson's pasture as a playing field. In 1905 a committee of officers bought Joe Holmes's cranberry bog and built the field at a cost of $600 for the land and improvements, naming it in honor of Rear Admiral Robley D. Evans, Commander of the Atlantic Squadron. Six battleships sent working parties and in two days they created a quarter-mile running track with a baseball diamond in the center and laid out lines for a 100-yard dash. Tents were erected and marked with the ships' pennants, and 2000 "jackies" (an old British term for seamen then in use) attended the festivities, which proved to be a great success.

During the summer, however, the fleet increased to 20 ships, putting more than 4000 men ashore on Sundays. Though generally very well behaved, a few sailors became rambunctious. They had obtained the "villainous Portuguese poison at a brush shack located between the Hennery and the Standpipe," according to a later report in the *Advocate*. This gave five local clergymen an opportunity to complain that Sunday blue laws were being flouted. Together with the three local selectmen, on September 10, 1905, they wrote to Admiral Evans

objecting to sailors playing on the field on Sundays. Some additional complaints about gunnery practice shattering windows were also made and a controversy erupted, continuing well into the next year. *Advocate* editor Hopkins espoused the point of view that the clergy were really angry because so many people were going to the games instead of to church and that a few drunken sailors were exposing the lack of enforcement of Provincetown's antiliquor laws. The officials continued their fuss until May 1906, when Admiral Evans (known as "Fighting Bob" for his daring and decisiveness in action) decided to call only briefly at Provincetown and proceed on to other ports where his men were more welcome. At that point, the town's businessmen tried to invite the squadron back, but only one ship, the *Louisiana*, spent 30 days in the harbor during 1906, the remainder only coming for a day or two at a time.

89. The Wessells Funeral. Though his death resulted from an accidental drowning in Provincetown Harbor, Coxswain Klass Wessells was considered the first local casualty of the Spanish-American War and was therefore provided a military funeral on June 6, 1898 by the Provincetown G.A.R. Post, seen here escorting the body along Standish Street to the cemetery.

89

Lives Saved

90. The Highland Life Saving Station. In 1871 Congress created the Life Saving Service in an effort to stem the great loss of life from shipwrecks. On the Cape alone, the official report lists 540 wrecks from 1880 to 1903. Thirteen stations, located about five to six miles apart, were established on the ocean side of Cape Cod. Each was manned by seven men—six surfmen and a keeper—who patrolled the beach from dusk to dawn (for 24 hours in bad weather). After 30 years of service the men were retired with two-thirds pay. In 1915 the Revenue Cutter Service and the Life Saving Service merged to become the U.S. Coast Guard.

The Highland Life Saving Station was built in 1872 in a hollow close to the beach below Highland Light. To the right of the station's main building are the stable and a pile of hay for Nellie, the horse that hauled the lifeboat or the carriage for the captain's trips between the station and town. Around 1901, when this photograph was taken, the captain was Edwin P. Worthen, who had come to Truro in 1844 at the age of seven. He had followed the sea until his appointment as keeper the year the station was built, making him at that time the longest-serving keeper in the United States. The cliffs along the patrol area from the Highland Station rise at points nearly 100 feet above the beach. At several points, the surfmen had ropes extending from top to bottom by which they could climb to the top at times of high tide.

91. Ballston Beach and the Pamet Life Saving Station. The cottages, a community building and a bowling alley were constructed in 1891 by Sheldon W. Ball, a New Yorker, and were listed as the Ballston Beach Inn in the 1901 directory. The community building, at the middle of this photograph of ca.1902, had a dining room supplied by a concessionaire on the main floor, as well as a ballroom. A porch ran around the upper floor, which contained lodgings for those working at the inn. Water, pumped by a windmill, was stored in large wooden cisterns, one of which is seen to the left of the cottages. In his published recollection of Truro of that era, Anthony L. Marshall recalls that the cottages primarily attracted a New York clientele who came for the entire season, many of whom returned over a period of five generations. By 1913, kitchens and indoor plumbing were provided and the community building, no longer needed, was dismantled, as was the bowling alley. According to Mr. Marshall, the cottages were moved seven times because of erosion of the bluff. In the 1960s, Ballston Beach became part of the Cape Cod National Seashore. In line with their policy of returning the area to a natural state, the cottages were torn down, the last in 1970.

92. The Pamet Life Saving Station. Four crew members pose in their painting gear, in a photograph probably taken on a Monday, the day in the weekly routine scheduled for putting the station and its equipment in order. They have been tentatively identified as Isaiah (Isaac) Hatch of Truro, with a total of nine years' service at the station, Richard F. Honey and George Paine, both of Truro and both with 12 years' service and Alonzo Nickerson of Harwich, a five-year veteran. The station's two Monomoy-model lifeboats can be seen just inside the double doors of the main building, which was usually painted a dark red for easy visibility from sea. The ramp allowed easy maneuvering of the boats and other equipment.

In addition to the rooms for the boats and beach equipment, the building also had a general room and a combination mess–sitting room. On the floor above were a room where the crew slept and another, also used for storage, with cots for rescued persons. The cupola above served as a daytime lookout tower. When the station was built in 1872, it stood several hundred feet from the high-water mark. By the time this photograph was taken (ca. 1901) and used as one of the original illustrations in J. B. Dalton's *Lifesavers of Cape Cod* (1902), the sea had made inroads into the sand dunes so that the buildings stood less than 100 feet from high water. The area is one of extensive sandbars and shallow water; station records detailed many disasters, including one in which three ships were wrecked at one time.

93. The Peaked Hill Bars Life Saving Station from the Southeast. The Peaked Hill Bars Life Saving Station was located near one of the most infamous stretches of shoreline on the Cape, between Highland Light and Wood End. Literally hundreds of ships foundered on these bars, from the first recorded, the British 64-gun frigate *Somerset* in 1778, to the *Jason*, the last full-rigged ship to go aground, in 1893. In November 1880, three members of the lifesaving crew here were lost during a rescue effort.

The station's two lifeboats, one four-oared, the other five-, can be seen in this photograph of 1904, as well as some of the other equip-

ment, which included two sets of beach apparatus, breeches buoys and a practice boat.

The station has also remained in memory as the home for several years of playwright Eugene O'Neill, who bought one of the old buildings after the government gave up the site. The 1925 *Literary Digest* described his house at Peaked Hill as "little changed from its former uses. The playwright's study is reached by a companionway draped with mackerel seines. The desk was made by men of the Coast Guard of walnut and mahogany salvaged from wrecks. A captain's chair, glazed red, does duty." Over the years erosion wore away the bluff until the building stood at its edge. During the 1938 hurricane it fell into the sea.

94. The Crew of the Peaked Hill Bars Life Saving Station. This photograph was used as another original illustration for J. B. Dalton's *Lifesavers of Cape Cod*, though Mr. Snow is not credited. (This is the only photograph in Mr. Snow's collection which has any technical information accompanying it. The envelope reads: "very cloudy 5 o'clock f 16 i sec."). Surfmen were numbered from 1 to 7 according to their competency and trustworthiness and could rise in rank by seniority or promotion. These surfmen, left to right, were: Levi A. Kelley of Provincetown, at the station since 1884; James F. Fish of East Boston, in service for 22 years; William D. Carlos of Provincetown, at that time a lifesaver for five years; Charles A. Higgins of Provincetown, a seven-year veteran; William E. Silvia, a former sailor and fisherman who was beginning his lifesaving work at the age of 32; and Benjamin R. Kelley of Truro, also at the station for 18 years and, at 57, the oldest crew member. Seated is Captain William W. Cook, in the service for 20 years, six as keeper at Peaked Hill. Born in Provincetown in 1852, he had gone to sea as a whaler, during which time he had gained wide experience in handling boats under the most adverse conditions. When going to a wreck in the surfboat, he used a 21-foot steering oar, the same kind he had used as a whaleman, and attributed to it his great success in handling the boat under the worst conditions of wind and wave.

95. The Wreck of the *Jennie C. May*. The three-masted schooner lies trapped on the inner bar at Peaked Hill Bars in 1902, after being driven over the outer bar. Her crew was rescued by the men of the Peaked Hill Bars Life Saving Station, but the ship was a total loss.

96. The End of the *Jennie C. May*. The surf pounds at all that remains of the ship. Her cargo of lath, it is certain, did not go to waste.

97. The Remains of the *Cathie C. Berry*. According to J. W. Dalton in *Lifesavers of Cape Cod*, the schooner was stranded at Peaked Hill during a terrific gale sometime in 1900–01. The lifesavers launched their boat and went to her aid, only to find her abandoned.

98. Long Point Light from the East. Long Point Light stands 36 feet above the water, virtually at the tip of Cape Cod on the southwest side of the entrance to Provincetown Harbor. Established in 1827, the station, shown here ca. 1905, was rebuilt in 1875. At that time it showed a fixed white light of 2900 candlepower visible for 12 miles. The light is now a fixed green. The structure to the right of the lighthouse supported a machine-operated bell that gave the fog signal: two quick successive strokes, then one after half a minute, followed by a longer interval. Over the years drifting sand has filled in and over the rock breakwater, which is now visible only from time to time, while the sandy tip of the Cape has extended itself so that Long Point Light now stands a considerable distance from the end.

From 1818 until the advent of the Civil War, a community of fishermen and people engaged in the manufacture of salt was established on Long Point. In its heyday, about the late 1840s, 38 families comprising over 200 people resided there permanently. More than 60 children attended a schoolhouse built for them on the point. About 1850 the first families moved off, the exodus continuing until 1861, when only two houses and the school remained. Almost all of the houses were floated on scows from Long Point and placed in the area then known as Gull Hill (now called Point Street).

Not far from the lighthouse, at a place called Herring Cove, was Nickerson's Whale and Menhaden Oil Works. Begun in 1886, the factory owned a steamer for catching whales and seines and seiners for obtaining menhaden. Expanded over the next three years to include a 400-foot-long wharf and equipment for making fertilizer, it was described as "one of the most perfect plants of its kind," employing during the season 25–30 workers and circulating yearly about $10,000 in town. Tourists were invited to tour the plant. Unfortunately, the factory did not prosper and the *Advocate* of 1908 reported:

> The boiler house of the oil and fertilizer plant maintained a few years ago at Herring Cove disappeared some time ago, but the boilers still remain on the site. [In 1886] the boiler house stood 500 feet from high-water mark, it is said. The bank on which the boilers stand at present is but a little removed from the sea, the boilers being within 15 feet of the water at high tide, this showing that the ocean has encroached upward of 450 feet at that point during the last 21 years.

99. The Race Point Life Saving Station. Outside of the building in this view of ca. 1900, one of the station's lifeboats sits in its cradle, the special wide wheels with iron edges for easy hauling through the sand clearly visible. The coast at Race Point is very treacherous: 92 vessels had met disaster near this station in the 15 years prior to 1902. The surfman in the photo was probably George H. Burch, the No. 2 man, a Provincetown native who was about 50 at the time and had served at Race Point for 15 years. About the horse, J. W. Dalton wrote: "[It] takes kindly to the work of dragging the heavy beach apparatus and surf boat through the sands. . . . [It] is the pet of all the surfmen, and seems to enjoy having visitors call to see him." The photograph was yet another originally used to illustrate *Lifesavers of Cape Cod*, which carries an advertisement from Campbell's Livery Stable in Provincetown: "We furnish careful drivers to accompany tourists to the Life-Saving Stations and all other points of interest."

100. Wood End Lighthouse. The light, seen here ca. 1905, was built in 1872 and stands near the entrance to Provincetown Harbor, 45 feet above the water. It can be seen for 12 miles. The light is a 15-second flashing red. According to early explorers and descriptions given by the Pilgrims in 1620, the land in Provincetown was well wooded. The name given to this area, not far from the end of Long Point, preserves the tradition that the forest once extended to the edge of the sea.

101. The Wood End Life Saving Station. In their dark dress uniforms and caps, the crew and captain pose in January 1900. The captain was Isaac Green Fisher (1838–1901), a former whaler who was keeper of the Peaked Hill Bars Station for 20 years, during which time he rescued hundreds of shipwrecked seafarers. Others tentatively identified are: No. 1, William Sparrow; No. 4, Frank C. Wager; No. 6, Willie F. Eldredge. On December 1 of each year, a winter surfman was added to the usual crew of a keeper and six surfmen, who were hired on the basis of their seaman's experience and ability, their good character and habits. Because of the rigorous nature of the work they had to undergo a physical examination once a year. They were paid $65 a month and normally worked a six-day week, taking weekly turns at cooking. At night the men patrolled the beach, in four watches between sunset and sunrise, and during the day in foggy or stormy weather. The stations were manned from August 1 to June 1, the captain living at the station year-round so that he could summon the crew in case of an emergency. All of the stations were connected to Provincetown by telephone.

99

100

101

102

102. A Lifeboat Drill. The crews of the lifesaving stations had a regular routine to follow each week. On Tuesdays they practiced launching and landing the lifeboats, as they are seen here, dressed in their white uniforms and cork life jackets. The surfboats were of heavy construction, weighing from 700 to 1000 pounds. Weather and surf conditions permitting, they were hauled to the launching site on a wheeled cradle by the station's horse. "Few sights are more impressive than the surf-boat plowing its way through the breakers, at times riding on top of the surge, at others held in suspension before the roaring tumultuous wall of water, or darting forth as the comber breaks and crumbles, obedient to the oars of the impassive life savers," wrote J. W. Dalton.

103. Wreckage at Union Wharf, from the West, After the Portland Gale. 104. Union Wharf, from the East, After the Portland Gale. The severe storm of November 26–27, 1898 has forever been memorialized as the Portland Gale, following the loss of the steamer *Portland*, with all 150–200 aboard, about seven miles northeast of Highland Light. During the same storm Provincetown lost 20 of its 54 wharves and hardly a boat in the harbor escaped without some damage. Union Wharf, one of the town's best and busiest, was built in 1831; a marine railway was added to it in 1852. In the 1880s Andrew T. Williams ran a ship chandlery on the wharf dealing in ship's stores, coal, wood, flour, groceries, seaman's outfits, paints and oils. Charles A. and Artemus P. Hannum were sailmakers there.

105. East Along the Shore from Gull Hill, Before the Portland Gale. A view taken in the far West End near the Red Inn looks toward Union, Paine and Central Wharves before the Portland Gale.

106. And After the Gale. A view from almost the same point below Gull Hill reveals the loss of buildings and wharves.

107. The Coast Guard Cutter *Morrill*. The ship was driven ashore in Provincetown after she lost her starboard anchor and her port anchor failed to hold during a southeast gale on November 16, 1926. The vessel did considerable damage to Pickert's fish plant at Cornell Wharf and practically demolished a small pavilion dock, but inspection of the hull revealed no damage and the *Morrill* was pulled clear three days later, proceeding to Railroad Wharf under her own steam. Two years later, having been in use since 1889, she was sold out of the service.

107

Bibliography

Cook, Lurana H., *et al., Provincetown Massachusetts Cemetery Inscriptions,* Heritage Books, Inc., Bowie, Maryland, 1980.

Dalton, J. W., *Lifesavers of Cape Cod,* The Barta Press, Boston, Massachusetts, 1902. (Reprinted by the Chatham Press, Old Greenwich, Connecticut, 1967.)

Deyo, Simeon L. (ed.), *History of Barnstable County, Massachusetts,* H. W. Blake & Co., New York, 1890.

Ferguson, Leonard W., *Cape Cod Collection Unit No. 2,* Salt Lake City, 1983.

The First Resident Directory of Provincetown, Mass. W. F. Richardson & Co., South Framingham, Mass., 1886.

Fisher, Charles E., *The Story of the Old Colony Railroad* (revised and enlarged edition), Frank P. Dubiel, Fall River, Massachusetts, 1974.

Hatch, Mellen C. M., *The Log of Provincetown and Truro on Cape Cod,* Provincetown, Massachusetts, 1939.

Jennings, Herman A., *Provincetown; or, Odds and Ends from the Tip End,* Yarmouth, Massachusetts, 1890.

Lawson, Evelyn, *Yesterday's Cape Cod* (No. 11 in Seemann's Historic Cities Series), E. A. Seemann Publishing, Inc., Miami, Florida, 1975.

Marshall, Anthony L., *Truro, Cape Cod, As I Knew It,* Vantage Press, New York, 1974.

Nordhoff, Charles, "Cape Cod, Nantucket and the Vineyard," *Harper's New Monthly Magazine,* June 1875, pages 52–66.

Provincetown Historical Association, Inc., *Provincetown Trapboat Fishing: The End of an Era,* Provincetown, Massachusetts, 1978.

Quinn, William P., *Shipwrecks Around Cape Cod,* Lower Cape Publishing, Orleans, Massachusetts, 1973.

Resident and Business Directory of Cape Cod, Mass., A. E. Foss Publishing Co., South Framingham, Massachusetts, 1901.

Seckler, Dorothy Gees, "History of the Provincetown Art Colony," in *Provincetown Painters, 1890's–1970's,* Everson Museum of Art, Syracuse, New York, 1977.

Small, Isaac Morton, *Just a Little Bit About the Lower Cape,* North Truro, Massachusetts, 1926.

Smith, Nancy W. Paine, *The Provincetown Book,* Tolman Print, Inc., Brockton, Massachusetts, 1922.

Index

This index lists persons, businesses, associations, publications, buildings, ships, constructions, monuments and wharves mentioned in the captions to the illustrations. Street names, neighborhoods, rivers and other sites are not included. The numbers used are those of the illustrations.